Early Canada
Explorers

Heather C. Hudak

Editor

Weigl

CALGARY
www.weigl.com

Published by Weigl Educational Publishers Limited
6325 10 Street SE
Calgary, Alberta, Canada
T2H 2Z9

Website: www.weigl.com
Copyright ©2007 Weigl Educational Publishers Limited

Library and Archives Canada Cataloguing in Publication Data

Explorers / editor: Heather Hudak.
(Early Canada)
Includes index.
ISBN 1-55388-240-7 (bound)
ISBN 1-55388-241-5 (pbk.)
1. Explorers—Canada—Biography—Textbooks. 2. Canada—
Discovery and exploration—Textbooks. I. Hudak, Heather C., 1975–
II. Series: Early Canada (Calgary, Alta.)
FC300.E965 2006   917.104092'2   C2006-902489-8

Printed in Canada
1 2 3 4 5 6 7 8 9 0 10 09 08 07 06

We acknowledge the financial support of the Government of Canada
through the Book Publishing Industry Development Program (BPIDP)
for our publishing activities.

Photograph and Text Credits
Every reasonable effort has been made to trace ownership and to
obtain permission to reprint copyright material. The publishers would
be pleased to have any errors or omissions brought to their attention so
that they may be corrected in subsequent printings.

Library and Archives Canada: pages 35, 43; **North Wind Picture
Archives:** pages 18, 23.

Project Coordinator
Leia Tait

Designer
Warren Clark

All of the Internet URLs
given in the book were
valid at the time of
publication. However, due
to the dynamic nature of
the Internet, some
addresses may have
changed, or sites may have
ceased to exist since
publication. While the
author and publisher regret
any inconvenience this may
cause readers, no
responsibility for
any such changes can be
accepted by either the
author or the publisher.

Contents

Introduction

Learning about the past is a bit like putting a puzzle together.

Canada is a large country with several geographic regions. The climate, land, and **resources** of these areas shaped the experiences of the country's earliest explorers. In turn, their explorations helped determine the path that settlement would take in early Canada. For this reason, their discoveries are still celebrated today.

Learning about people and events in history can help people better understand Canada in the present. However, finding out what happened in the past and why it happened can be a challenge. In order to study the past, historians must piece together history from many different sources. Sometimes, they listen to the stories people tell. Often, they read historical **documents**. Many explorers who came to early Canada wrote about their visits in journals and letters to their families. They also sent reports to their **monarchs**. Some of these documents still exist. From these records, historians can learn about the experiences of early explorers.

Without cameras, explorers to early Canada relied on their own artistic skills to depict the new people and places they saw. They sketched and painted the plants and animals they found in the North American wilderness. Sometimes, explorers included

Theodore de Bry's engravings in *Americae Tertia Pars* show European perceptions of unexplored waters off the shores of the Americas.

themselves and their activities in their drawings. These images can tell historians a great deal about the early explorers and how they viewed the new land that they visited.

Historians and archaeologists also study objects from the past to learn more about the people who made and used them. For example, navigational tools used by the explorers can reveal important facts about their lives on board discovery ships.

Learning about the past is a bit like putting a puzzle together. Pieces of information from different sources fit together to form a picture. Sometimes pieces are missing, so the picture is not complete. Then, historians must try to guess what really happened.

Many explorers preferred small ships because they were easier to handle.

FURTHER UNDERSTANDING

Archaeologists

Archaeologists study objects from the past, called artifacts. From artifacts, archaeologists can learn the customs and traditions of the people who made and used them. They can also determine how long ago people might have lived in a certain area.

Forces of Exploration

About 1,000 years ago, Europeans began to show an interest in exploration. They looked beyond the borders of Europe. They began to wonder about the lands and people that existed in other parts of the world.

Starting in the twelfth century, the desire to explore began to affect many different peoples from all across Europe. Different groups felt the need to travel for various reasons. Some, such as the **Norse** peoples of northern Europe, lived in overcrowded places. Years of war had also taken a toll on the land. A few daring individuals took to the oceans in search of new lands where they would be able to farm.

A few centuries later, the desire for wealth and luxury goods led other groups, including the British, French, and Spanish, to begin exploring outside Europe. Explorers from these countries sought routes to distant and unknown lands. They hoped to find new people to trade with, who could supply them with luxury items such as silk, spices, and other unknown riches.

Still other groups were motivated by the desire to improve their knowledge of the world. They sought to learn about distant peoples and places, and to share European ideas with those who knew nothing of them.

Star anise is native to Asia. European explorers searched for a new route to the East in order to obtain such spices.

6

Life in Europe

About 600 years ago, life in Europe was very different than it is today. Great Britain, France, and Spain were ruled by kings. The king was the most powerful person in the country. He owned all the land and had control over everyone. To defend his domain, the king divided his land into smaller holdings that were ruled by nobles. Nobles were wealthy individuals who held official titles and served on the king's council. In return for use of the king's land, noblemen pledged him their **allegiance**. They paid the king rent in the form of crops, goods, or money. In times of war, which were frequent, nobles also supplied the king with an army.

The rest of the population was made up of peasants. Peasants did not own any land of their own. Instead, they lived on land supplied by the nobles. In return for shelter and protection, peasants were required to farm the land. They provided the nobles with free labour, crops, and service whenever it was demanded. They also paid a variety of taxes to their noble lords.

For both nobles and peasants, religion was a very important part of daily life. Christianity served as the basis for European society. People attended church daily, and most noble lands had their own chapels and priests for this purpose. Most Europeans belonged to the Roman Catholic church, and religious

European peasants had to provide their lords with some of their crops in exchange for a place to live.

leaders played an important role in politics. Bishops and archbishops often served on the king's council. The Pope, who was the leader of the church, was one of the most powerful people in Europe.

FURTHER UNDERSTANDING

Christianity

Christianity is a religion based on the life and teachings of Jesus of Nazareth, also called the Christ, or the Anointed One of God. It began in the first century and spread throughout Europe over the next 1,000 years. When European explorers travelled to new areas of the world, they taught Christianity to the people they met. Today, it is one of the largest religions in the world.

An Unknown Land

During prehistoric times, the land developed into the continent it is today.

Although European explorers had not sailed west before, the land they came to in the late fifteenth century was ancient. Some rocks in the earth had existed for nearly 4 billion years. During prehistoric times, the land developed into the continent it is today. North America reached its present size and shape about 600 million years ago. Over the next few million years, the land's interior features developed. Mountains lifted, valleys sunk, and rivers were formed. Plants and animals also came to inhabit the land.

Many Aboriginal groups believe their ancestors always lived on the land now known as Canada. However, scientists believe that the first people may have arrived on the continent more than 14,000 years ago. They came to North

At the time of its discovery, early Canada had many ancient forests.

America from Asia, travelling across a land bridge called Beringia, which connected the two continents. Early people may also have arrived in North America by crossing the ocean on boats from Australia and Europe.

These ancient peoples were the ancestors of Canada's **Aboriginal Peoples**. Once they arrived on the continent, they moved around the continent for thousands of years.

Over time, they adapted to the land and climate of different regions. Early Aboriginal Peoples developed into a number of diverse groups. By the time Europeans arrived in North America, each group had its own way of life, its own language, its own spiritual beliefs, and its own laws. The way different groups lived was linked to the different types of land they lived on.

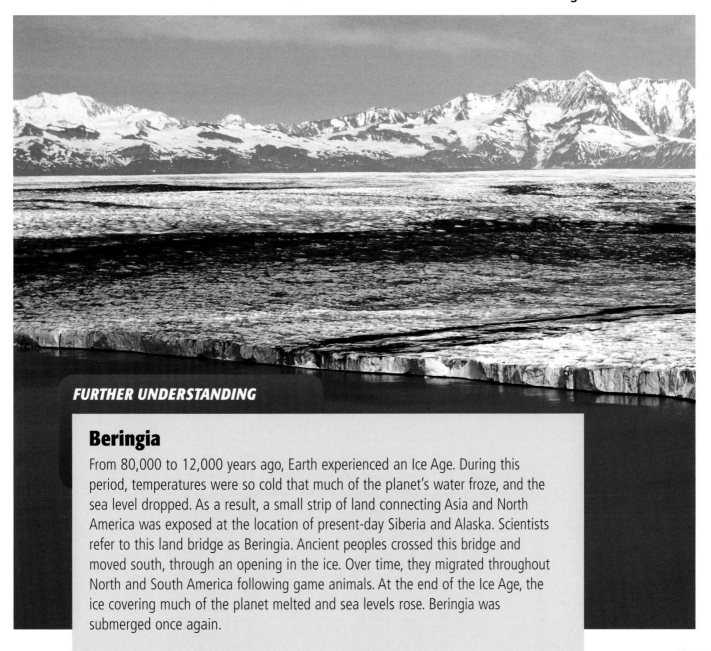

The Bering Glacier in Alaska is a massive sheet of ice left over from the Ice Age.

FURTHER UNDERSTANDING

Beringia

From 80,000 to 12,000 years ago, Earth experienced an Ice Age. During this period, temperatures were so cold that much of the planet's water froze, and the sea level dropped. As a result, a small strip of land connecting Asia and North America was exposed at the location of present-day Siberia and Alaska. Scientists refer to this land bridge as Beringia. Ancient peoples crossed this bridge and moved south, through an opening in the ice. Over time, they migrated throughout North and South America following game animals. At the end of the Ice Age, the ice covering much of the planet melted and sea levels rose. Beringia was submerged once again.

THE MEANING OF ABORIGINAL NAMES

By the time European explorers first found North America, the land had been occupied by Aboriginal Peoples for thousands of years. Many different groups lived all across what is now Canada. Peoples such as the Inuit, Beothuk, and the Dene occupied parts of the Canadian Arctic and Subarctic. The Bella Coola and their neighbours inhabited lands along the Northwest Coast. Numerous groups, including the Blackfoot Nation, made their homes in the Plains region. Still others, including the Kootenay and the Iroquois, occupied the Interior Plateau and the Northeastern Woodlands. Each different group had its own identity, which was often symbolized by a unique name.

The Meaning of Group Names

Each group of Aboriginal Peoples had a unique name. Often, the name had a meaning that symbolized something important about the group. For example, *Chipewyan* means "pointed skins." This was a reference to the special cut of these peoples' clothes. Sometimes, a group's name was given to them by another group. Often, these names were offensive. For instance, the name Sarcee means "not nice." The Sarcee were given this name by their Blackfoot neighbours. The following list includes the meaning of many other Aboriginal groups' names.

Assiniboin	Beothuk	Blood	Chilcotin	Dog Rib	Haida
"people that cook with hot stones"	"human"	named for the red paint that decorated their clothing	the inhabitants of "young man's river"	derived from a legend that says they were descended from a dog	"people"

Inuit	Iroquois	Kwakiutl	Lilloet	Mi'kmaq	Montagnais
"the people"	"human"	"beach on the other side of the river"	"wild onion"	"allies"	"mountaineer"

Naskapi	Neutral	Ojibwa	Ottawa	Peigan	Potawatomi
"rude, uncivilized people" (a name given to them by the Montagnais)	named for their neutrality during the Huron-Iroquois conflict	people whose moccasins have puckered seam	"traders"	"scabby" or poorly tanned hides	"people of the place of fire"

Sekani	Slave	Tahltan	Tobacco	Tsetsaut	Tsimshian
"people of the rocks" (Rocky Mountains)	named in contempt by the Cree	referred to the geography of the area in which the group lived	named after their main crop	"inland people"	"people of the Skeena River"

Wenday (Wyandot)
"islanders" or "dwellers on a peninsula"

Often, the name had a meaning that symbolized something important about the group.

Mapping the Route

European explorers began making maps of North America when they arrived on the continent.

Maps do more than show where cities and towns are located. They show the distances between places. They also show which parts of the world are water and which are land.

The earliest maps of Canada were drawn by Aboriginal Peoples. Some individuals memorized certain areas of land. When others wanted to travel, the mapmakers drew a map for them in sand or snow. Sometimes they drew maps on bark or animal hides.

European explorers began making maps of North America as soon as they arrived on the continent. Many early explorers relied on the knowledge of Aboriginal Peoples to help them map the areas they visited. The earliest maps often showed only the coastlines of the continent. Mapmakers left empty spaces when they were unsure of the features of an area. As they travelled and learned more about the land, explorers added features to their maps, such as rivers, lakes, and mountains. Settlements and roads were also added to the maps once they were built.

Through their travels, many early explorers helped map North America one step at a time. The following map shows the places visited by the early explorers and some of their main routes.

— Norse

- Bjarni Herjulfsson of Iceland first saw North America when his ship travelled off course in AD 985.
- In 1000, Leif Eriksson built a settlement on the island that is now Newfoundland and Labrador. It failed within 15 years.
- The Norse explorers were the first Europeans to make contact with Aboriginal Peoples.

— John Cabot

- Cabot was an Italian explorer hired by the rulers of Great Britain to find a route to Asia.
- He left on his first voyage in 1497.
- Cabot claimed what is now Newfoundland and Labrador for Great Britain.

— João Fernandes

- Fernandes was a Portuguese sailor with links to Great Britain.
- He travelled to North America in 1499.
- Fernandes probably reached what is now Newfoundland and Labrador.

— Gaspar Corte-Real

- Corte-Real was a Portuguese explorer.
- He landed in what was probably Newfoundland and Labrador in 1501.

— João Alvares Fagundes

- Fagundes was an explorer from Portugal.
- In 1520, he may have established a colony on Cape Breton Island.

Giovanni da Verrazzano

- Verrazzano was an Italian explorer hired by

European Explorers in North America

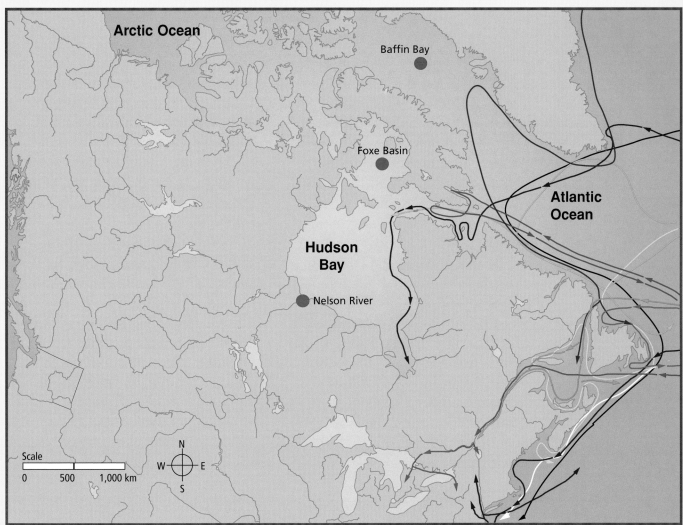

- the rulers of France to find a route to Asia.
- In 1524, Verrazzano sailed the coast of North America from Florida to Cape Breton Island.

Jacques Cartier

- Cartier was a master sailor from France.
- In 1534, Cartier explored the Gulf of St. Lawrence. He later visited Prince Edward Island and New Brunswick.

- Cartier claimed these areas for France.

Martin Frobisher

- Frobisher was an explorer from Great Britain.
- In 1576, he tried to find a route to Asia by sailing northwest around North America.
- Frobisher discovered what became known as Frobisher Bay.

Samuel de Champlain

- Champlain was an explorer from France.
- He explored the St. Lawrence River in 1603.
- Champlain set up French colonies at Port-Royal and Quebec.

Henry Hudson

- Hudson was a British explorer who followed in Frobisher's footsteps.
- In 1609, he searched for the Northwest Passage.

- Hudson explored what later became known as Hudson Bay.

Explorers in the Arctic

- After 1600, explorers from Great Britain led the exploration of Canada's North.
- Between 1612 and 1631, Thomas Button, Robert Bylot, William Baffin, and Luke Foxe explored the Canadian Arctic.

Arrival of the Norse

The story of
the Norse
discovery and
settlement of
North America
is full
of mystery.

One thousand years ago, the Norse lived in the northern areas of Europe, which today make up the countries of Iceland, Denmark, Norway, and Sweden. At the beginning of the ninth century, their homelands became overcrowded. The more daring Norse took to the oceans in search of new farmlands, adventure, and profit. They sailed the coasts of Europe in their sleek long ships called drakkars. The drakkars were decorated with striped sails and a carved dragon head on the prow, or the front, of the boat. These adventurers **plundered** towns along the coasts of the Atlantic Ocean and the North Sea. Most Europeans lived in fear of them.

In about 985, a Norseman named Bjarni Herjulfsson was blown off course while sailing from Iceland to Greenland. Heading westward, he became the first European to sight North America, sailing along the Atlantic coastline of eastern Canada before returning home.

A few years later, in about 1000, Leif Eriksson sailed in search of the lands Herjulfsson had seen. Eriksson and a crew of 35 men also reached the Atlantic coast of Canada. Experts believe he sailed the area near Baffin Island and then south along the

Historians believe Leif Eriksson may have reached Vinland by mistake while travelling from Norway to Greenland.

coast of what is now Newfoundland and Labrador. There, the group went ashore at a warm, wooded area, which they named Vinland. They built some houses and spent the winter exploring the area before sailing back to Greenland.

Around 1003, Leif's brother Thorvald returned to Vinland. He and his crew became the first Europeans to make contact with Aboriginal Peoples living there. However, their dealings were not peaceful. Thorvald was killed during a battle, and the surviving members of his crew returned to Greenland.

Within a few years, Thorfinn Karlsefni led another expedition to Vinland. His group of about 130 people stayed for three years. They maintained peace with Aboriginal Peoples for some time. Eventually, war again broke out between the two

groups. Shortly after, the Norse returned to Greenland.

The story of the Norse discovery and settlement of North America is full of mystery. At the time, no other Europeans seemed to know about the explorations of the Norse. According to historians, when Christopher Columbus set out on his well-known voyage across the Atlantic Ocean in 1492, most Europeans had never heard of Vinland.

L'Anse aux Meadows became a World Heritage Site in 1978.

FURTHER UNDERSTANDING

Vinland

Vinland was the first European settlement in North America. The exact location of the colony is not certain, but most experts believe that Norse ruins found at L'Anse aux Meadows in present-day Newfoundland and Labrador probably marks the location of Vinland. The settlement was named for the vines and berries the Norse found while exploring their new environment. Believing the berries to be grapes, they called the new land Vinland, or "Wineland." Historians believe that the fruits may actually have been cranberries.

The Age of Discovery

The fifteenth century was an exciting time in Europe.

For several centuries, the Norse were the only explorers to visit North America. At the time, most European countries were struggling with problems such as famine, disease, and war. Exploring other lands was of little interest to them. This did not change until the 1400s.

The fifteenth century was an exciting time in Europe. People's ideas about the world were changing. New technologies were invented, which made it possible for ships to sail farther than ever before. At the same time, Europeans were becoming more aware of other lands. They became more interested in knowledge, the arts, and the cultures of the world. This age of discovery lasted until about 1650. Today, it is referred to as the Renaissance.

During the Renaissance, Europeans became interested in discovering new trade opportunities and ways of obtaining fresh goods. The promise of riches made them eager to explore the unknown. They constructed larger, more seaworthy ships, and improved navigational devices such as the compass, **sextant**, and **astrolabe**, to make sailing easier.

Of special interest to explorers was finding a new route to Asia. Recent travellers to the Far East had returned with exotic silks and spices, and Europeans were eager to begin trading for these luxury goods in earnest.

Trade with Asia was difficult, however. Over land, goods were carried by camel caravans across mountains and deserts. This route was known as the Silk Road.

During the age of discovery, maps looked very different than they do today.

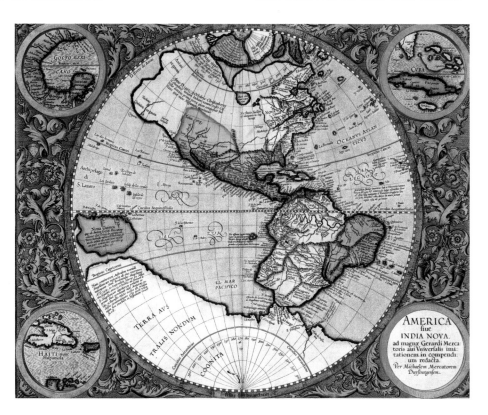

Travel by water was no easier. At ports on the Mediterranean Sea, traders paid expensive tolls to load their goods onto ships. The ships then had to sail around the southern tip of Africa before heading to Asia. The water route south of Africa was especially dangerous. It could take months, and even years, to complete. European explorers began to look for a faster route to Asia.

Until then, people had believed that the world was flat. If a ship sailed too far out to sea, they thought it would fall off the edge. During the Renaissance, a few navigators and scientists began to claim that the world was actually round. In 1492, a new map charting these theories appeared in Nuremberg, Germany. The map, called the Behaim Globe, showed a few scattered islands between Europe and Asia. Navigators reasoned that, if the world was indeed round, a shorter route to the Far East could be found across this "small" ocean. Many European countries, including Great Britain, Spain, and France, sent exploration teams across the Atlantic Ocean in search of this new route to Asia. Instead, they found the Americas.

Traders transported silk and other riches along the silk road.

FURTHER UNDERSTANDING

The Silk Road

The Silk Road was one of the most important trade routes in the world. For almost 2,000 years (200 BC–AD 1700), traders transported goods along the route from China to countries and empires around the Mediterranean Sea. The Silk Road was made up of three major routes and hundreds of smaller side roads. All of the routes at the eastern end of the road began in Xian, the capital of ancient China. The northern route led from China to the Black Sea. The central route led to Persia—now known as Iran—and the Mediterranean Sea. The southern route took traders through Afghanistan and Persia to India.

The Spice Trade

During the **Middle Ages**, Italian and Muslim traders controlled the Asian trade goods travelling to Europe. European countries did not want to pay the high prices charged by the Italians and Muslims for silk, spices, and other luxury items shipped from Asia. To avoid paying these high prices, some European countries funded expeditions to find a sea route from Asia to Europe. The spice trade is considered to be at least partially responsible for European exploration in the fifteenth and sixteenth centuries.

Columbus Sets Sail

On October 12, 1492, Columbus and his crew finally landed on an island in the Caribbean.

Several times in September 1492, sailors on board Columbus' ships spotted vegetation floating in the ocean and birds flying overhead—signs that land was nearby.

During the Age of Discovery, European kings and queens invested large amounts of money in exploration. They hoped to gain power and riches through the discovery of new lands and resources. At the time, Portugal and Spain were two of the strongest seafaring nations. They led the search to find an ocean passage to the Far East.

The rulers of Spain hired Christopher Columbus, an Italian navigator, to find a shorter route westward across the Atlantic Ocean. In 1492, Columbus and his crew set sail in three small ships called the *Nina,* the *Pinta,* and the *Santa Maria*.

Columbus estimated that the voyage would take about one week. Instead, it took 71 days. On October 12, 1492, Columbus and his crew finally landed on an island in the Caribbean. Columbus thought he had found the East Indies. In later voyages, he sailed along the coasts of Central and South America, all the time believing that he had succeeded in finding a new route to Asia. Although Columbus was mistaken, his explorations of the Americas and the trading that followed helped Spain become the wealthiest nation in Europe at the time.

FURTHER UNDERSTANDING

East Indies

The term "Indies" was first used in the 1400s. At the time it referred to southeastern Asia—including India, Burma, Thailand, Laos, Cambodia, and Vietnam—as well as the Philippines and the Malay Archipelago. Columbus believed he had landed in the Indies when he discovered America. As a result, he named the islands he discovered the "Caribbean Indies." Today, the Caribbean Indies are known as the West Indies, while the East Indies primarily refer to the islands of the Malay Archipelago.

Was Columbus a Hero?

Like all forms of storytelling, history is coloured by the knowledge and attitudes of the person telling it. As time passes, attitudes and values change. More information may also be revealed. In 1993, the 500th anniversary of Columbus' first voyage created a great deal of controversy. Decide whether you think Columbus' achievements are worthy of special recognition.

Reading 1

On August 3, 1492, Columbus sailed from Palos with three well-equipped and seaworthy ships. The enterprise was intelligently organised as the results proved. On October 12, the ships came in sight of land. Columbus went ashore and claimed possession in the name of the Spanish crown. He sailed among the islands and explored Cuba and Haiti.

Columbus returned to Spain believing the islands were in the neighbourhood of the Asiatic mainland. Although Columbus made three more trips to the "Indies" before his death, it is probable that he never realised he had not reached the east.
[Adapted from Joseph Reither, *World History at a Glance,* New York: Garden City Publishing, 1942, p. 228.]

Reading 2

Finally, and speaking only of what has taken place on this voyage, which has been so hasty, their Highnesses may see that I shall give them all the gold they require, if they will give me but very little assistance; spices also, and cotton, as much as their Highnesses shall command to be shipped; and...slaves, as many as their Highnesses shall command to be shipped.
[Excerpt of a letter from Christopher Columbus to Louis Santangel, a Spanish government official, written in February 1493.]

Reading 3

Recent research into the life and times of Christopher Columbus has somewhat diminished his heroic image as an isolated visionary by placing him in the context of a broad wave of exploration. Historians continue to praise his courage, persistence, and maritime ability. Critics point to his cruelty, his poor administration of [the lands he discovered], and his role in beginning the exploitation of the Americas.
[Excerpt from *The World Book Encyclopedia,* 1992, p.864.]

Reflecting on this issue:

1. In the United States, Christopher Columbus is honoured with a holiday in October. Discuss whether Columbus should be credited with the "discovery" of America.
2. In 1992, some groups in North America held mock trials of Columbus. They felt it was time to draw attention to his treatment of the Aboriginal Peoples of South America. Hold a trial of Columbus in your classroom. Be prepared to fully defend your side.
3. In 1986, *The World Book Encyclopedia* described Columbus as a hero to whom the world owed a great debt. Why might their 1992 description of Columbus, as seen in reading 3, have changed? What should we keep in mind when we read any account of an historical event?

LIFE ABOARD THE DISCOVERY SHIPS

Exploring the oceans was difficult work. It required careful preparation and endurance. Explorers had to choose a route before setting sail. Ships had to be built to withstand the constant strains of ocean waves. Supplies had to be packed to sustain the crew members on long journeys. Crew members had to cope with uncomfortable living conditions and tough physical labor to keep the ships operational. The life of an explorer was certainly not for everyone.

Most of the ships built for discovery voyages were either caravels or galleons. Spanish and Portuguese shipbuilders constructed the first caravels in the late 1400s. These ships had both square and triangular sails. Most were about 20 metres long and could carry about 50 tonnes of cargo. Caravels were built mostly of oak and were held together with wooden pegs and rope. The planks were sealed with oakum—a kind of rope—and waterproofed with tar. Caravels were popular sailing ships because they were lightweight and moved at great speeds in the wind.

Galleons were much larger than caravels. Most had three **masts**—two with square sails, and one with a triangular sail. Galleons were originally designed as warships. They were heavily armed with cannons and had several decks that could serve as fighting platforms. Below deck, there was space to carry large amounts of cargo. Despite their great size, galleons could also reach rapid speeds. They were frequently used to make long journeys across the ocean in the 1500s and 1600s.

Living conditions on board ships of discovery were cramped and filthy. Only the captain had his own quarters. The rest of the crew slept where they could find room. Most of the space below deck was taken up with food stores and other supplies.

Crowds gathered to watch the early discovery ships set sail.

It was difficult to store enough food to feed the crews for such long ocean voyages. Meals consisted of dried or salted meat and fish, as well as biscuits, rice, dried peas, cheese, garlic, and onions. The diet was high in salt and lacking in fresh fruits and vegetables. Sailors often became ill with a disease called scurvy because they did not have any vitamin C in their diets. Scurvy caused their skin and gums to rot and their teeth to fall out.

Since ships were designed to prevent water from seeping through the wooden frame, storage areas below deck were poorly **ventilated**. Despite efforts to make the ships airtight, water still leaked on board. The combination of moisture and stale air often caused food to spoil. Rats and insects infested food supplies. Even staples, such as biscuits, grains, and flour, swarmed with insects or were covered with mould long before the end of the voyage. Storing water was also a problem. Even though ships were surrounded by ocean on all sides, the salt water was unsuitable to drink. Crews stored fresh water on board in barrels. These often sprung leaks, depleting the critical supply of fresh water. On long journeys, fresh water also spoiled inside the barrels. For this reason, beer was the main beverage. Crew members had to wait until they landed on dry land to seek fresh water.

Ships were unclean. The stench was often overwhelming, and it filled all the living spaces. Poor sanitary habits meant that illness spread rapidly between crew members. Many died.

Despite these difficulties, many explorers sailed westward during the age of discovery. Their desire for adventure and riches proved stronger than any dread of hardship or fear of the unknown.

▼▼▼▼▼▼▼▼

Many explorers sailed westward during the age of discovery.

Since they were fast and easy to navigate, caravels made excellent ships for exploration.

John Cabot

News of Columbus' voyages spread across Europe. Another Italian sea captain, Giovanni Caboto, known as John Cabot in Great Britain, shared Columbus' dream of finding a western route to Asia. In 1496, Cabot received permission from King Henry VII of England to explore and claim for Great Britain all new lands he might discover. **Merchants** from Bristol, England, provided him with a ship and a crew.

In May 1497, Cabot and his crew of 18 sailed from Bristol on a ship called the *Matthew*. On June 24, after 54 days at sea, they sighted land. Believing they had arrived in the Far East, Cabot and his crew sailed along the coast of this new land. They eventually landed at what is now Newfoundland and Labrador, where Cabot became the first person to claim North American land for Great Britain. He planted the British flag in the soil before continuing his travels. Further along the coast, Cabot and his crew discovered an area where the waters were rich with cod. Today, this area is called the Grand Banks.

After about a month, Cabot returned to Great Britain to tell about his voyage. Although he had returned with neither spices nor silk, the merchants who had provided Cabot's ship were very

Cabot and his crew were amazed by the number of cod in the Grand Banks.

FURTHER UNDERSTANDING

Grand Banks

Located southeast of present-day Newfoundland and Labrador, the Grand Banks cover 500 kilometres of shallow water. They are known internationally for their fishing resources, especially cod. When Cabot and his crew first discovered the waters, they found so many fish that they could catch them just by lowering buckets into the water. Following Cabot's reports of the Grand Banks, numerous European fishers travelled to the area. They organized some of Newfoundland and Labrador's first settlements as places to prepare the fish for transport back to Europe.

pleased to hear that he had discovered new fishing grounds with plentiful cod. Cod was the least expensive and most popular fish to eat in Bristol.

King Henry VII rewarded Cabot with money and the title of great admiral. He also promised Cabot ships for another voyage to the "New Founde Land." In 1498, Cabot set sail with five ships.

On board were 300 crew members, a one-year supply of food, and items to trade. Soon after they left Bristol, Cabot's expedition was caught in a storm. One of the ships was damaged and returned to Bristol. The others were never heard from again. No one knows what happened to Cabot and his crew. Many historians believe they were lost at sea.

Early Fishing

After Cabot and his crew discovered the Grand Banks, sailors began to fish there every summer. They returned to Europe with their cargo **holds** filled with fish.

Fish was an important part of the European diet. Religious teachings forbade Christians to eat meat on Fridays and about 150 other holy days each year. Since fish was not considered meat, it was in great demand. Cod was popular because it did not spoil as quickly as other fish.

Since the voyage to the Grand Banks was so long, fishers had to preserve their catches before they headed home. French crews heavily salted the cod and stored it on their ships. The British did not have as much salt as the French, so they preserved their

fish by cleaning and lightly salting it before drying the fish in the Sun. They packed the dried cod in barrels that could be shipped virtually anywhere. The dried cod rarely spoiled.

Eventually, some British captains began to leave a few crew members on shore each winter. These individuals stayed behind in what is now

Fishermen cleaned, salted, dried, and stored their catches on structures called stages.

Newfoundland and Labrador to take care of the crew's fishing equipment. They built small settlements, and North America became their home.

The Portuguese in North America

King Manuel of Portugal sent several men to explore the lands that Cabot had visited.

Portuguese sailors had followed Christopher Columbus across the Atlantic. In 1494, Portugal signed a **treaty** with Spain, which granted them control over some parts of North and South America. News of John Cabot's travels to North America aroused fears that Great Britain would meddle in the North American lands already claimed by Portugal. King Manuel of Portugal sent several men to explore the lands that Cabot had visited.

Possibly the first of these was João Fernandes, a sailor with connections to Bristol. He was known by his rank of "lavrador," or landowner. In 1499, Fernandes sailed west with several Bristol merchants. Historians believe he reached Greenland in 1500, and possibly Labrador, which may

When Fernandes reached Greenland, he called it *Terra do Lavrador*. The name was later applied to what is now Labrador, in Canada's Atlantic region.

have been named after him. The following year, he was lost on another voyage to North America.

In 1500, King Manuel ordered another sailor, Gaspar Corte-Real, to visit what is now Newfoundland and Labrador. Corte-Real sighted Greenland, but was unable to reach land due to ice packs off the coast. In 1501, Corte-Real set sail again with three ships. He reached a coast where several rivers flowed out to the sea and pine trees grew as tall as ships' masts. Historians believe that this land was probably present-day Newfoundland and Labrador. Corte-Real and his crew captured about 60 Aboriginal men and women from the region before turning back. Two of the ships returned to Portugal in 1501, but Corte-Real's ship was lost at sea and never seen again.

Over time, Portuguese rulers began to focus on the spice trade with India, and their interest in exploring North America declined. One of the last major Portuguese voyages to North America occurred in 1520. João Alvares Fagundes explored the southern coast of Newfoundland and Labrador and possibly Nova Scotia. It is believed that he planned to start a **colony** in the area, but historians do not know if he succeeded. No evidence of a settlement has ever been found.

In 1497, Vasco da Gama was sent to solidify Portugal's trade routes in Asia. When da Gama successfully returned to Portugal, he was rewarded for his efforts.

FURTHER UNDERSTANDING

Portuguese Place Names

Although the Portuguese did not establish a permanent settlement in what was to become Canada, places such as Cape Race, Cape Spear, Cape Bonavista, and Cape Foggo bear names that date back to the Portuguese explorers.

Giovanni da Verrazzano

During the early 1500s, French ships joined other European fishing vessels in the annual harvest of cod from the Grand Banks. For many years, these Atlantic fishing grounds had attracted French sailors to the New World.

In the mid-1500s, the French king, Francis I, heard reports that Spain was becoming wealthy from the trade of spices and goods brought from Asia. He decided that France should enter into trade with Asia. He hired an Italian navigator, Giovanni da Verrazzano, to lead the French expedition to discover a route to Asia across the Atlantic.

Verrazzano was certain that he would find a middle passage to the Far East located somewhere between the newly discovered lands to the north and what is now the U.S. state of Florida. Wealthy European bankers supplied the funds for the expedition, and in 1523,

> Verrazzano was certain that he would find a middle passage to the Far East.

Verrazzano was born in Val di Greve, Italy, in 1480. He was killed on an expedition to Brazil, possibly in 1527.

Verrazzano left France with four ships. Heavy storms soon drove him back and forced him to revise his plans. In early 1524, he sailed a second time with only one ship, a crew of 50, and enough supplies for an 8-month voyage.

In March 1524, Verrazzano landed on the coast of North America, near what is now Florida. During the following weeks, he explored the entire coast as far north as Cape Breton Island. He was the first European to do so. Finding no passage, Verrazzano gave up his search. Before returning home, he claimed the entire eastern coast of North America for France.

FURTHER UNDERSTANDING

King Francis I of France

When Francis I sent Verrazzano on his expedition, there was more at stake than wealth. Throughout the Renaissance, Spain and France were frequently at war with each other. Francis I wanted to find a more direct route to Asia so that France could gain control of the spice trade and defeat its Spanish rival.

Tools of Navigation

The safety and success of early exploration relied heavily upon accurate navigation of the Atlantic Ocean. Navigators on board the discovery ships used a variety of techniques and tools to plot and maintain a course across the ocean.

To help determine the location of their ship and the direction that they travelled, sailors studied the size of ocean waves and watched the direction of the current. They observed the wind, which blew from various directions during different seasons. Some explorers even kept birds on their ships. When they were released at sea, the birds flew in the direction of land, and the explorers followed.

Ships were equipped with a variety of navigational tools. One of these was the compass. Compasses have a magnetic

Explorer Amerigo Vespucci used the position of the stars in the night sky to navigate the seas.

needle that always points north. The needle helped explorers determine what direction their ships were travelling.

Other important tools included the astrolabe, which was used to find the position of the Sun, the Moon, and stars in the sky. This information helped sailors calculate the latitude of their ships. The backstaff, or Davis quadrant, measured the height of the Sun. Like the astrolabe, it was also used to determine latitude. Ship movements and bad weather could distort the readings of both of these tools. Plotting a course and making sure a ship reached its destination was difficult work.

FURTHER UNDERSTANDING

Latitude

Latitude is how far north or south an object is located on Earth. It is measured from the equator, which is an invisible line that runs from east to west through the centre of Earth. Navigators calculated a ship's latitude to determine its position in the ocean. They used astrolabes, crossstaffs, and quadrants to help them find it.

Jacques Cartier

Despite the failure of early explorers to find a western route to Asia, Europeans continued to search. In 1534, the king of France, François I, hired Jacques Cartier to explore the new lands across the Atlantic Ocean. Cartier was a master sailor from St. Malo, France. Francis I hoped Cartier would be successful in finding a northwest passage to Asia.

Cartier left France on his first voyage to North America on April 30, 1534. It took his two ships 20 days to reach what is now Newfoundland and Labrador. Once there, Cartier sailed around the north end of the island, down the west side, and into the Gulf of St. Lawrence. He and his crew spent the summer looking for a route to Asia near the Gulf of St. Lawrence. In June, they discovered Prince Edward Island. In July, Cartier landed on a large outcrop of land known today as the Gaspé **Peninsula.** He raised a large cross on the shore and claimed the territory for France.

There, Cartier met a group of Iroquois who had come to fish on the coast. The Iroquois chief, Donnacona, was present. Cartier gave Donnacona knives, glass beads, combs, and tin rings as gifts. In return, Donnacona's people shared the food they had brought from their village, Stadacona. Cartier and his crew stayed in the area over the summer months. With winter approaching, however, it was time to return to France. Before

On his first voyage to the St. Lawrence River, Jacques Cartier sailed as far as Anticosti Island.

FURTHER UNDERSTANDING

The Northwest Passage

Early explorers of the Americas believed they had arrived in Asia. They were searching for a passage to the Pacific Ocean. Some focussed on what they called the Northwest Passage. These explorers believed that Asia could be reached more quickly by travelling through the Arctic region of North America. For more than 300 years, explorers travelled northwest through the land and waters of North America trying to find a route to the Pacific Ocean. Although the desired route was not found until 1845, numerous explorers discovered many other important places along the way, including the St. Lawrence River, Baffin Bay, Davis Strait, and Frobisher Bay.

leaving, Cartier took captive Donnacona's two sons, Taignoagny and Domagaya. With the two young men on board, Cartier's ships arrived back in France on September 4, 1534.

The following year, Cartier sailed for North America once again. This time he had three ships and a crew of 110 people, including Donnacona's two sons. Once the ships crossed the ocean, Domagaya and Taignoagny showed Cartier the route up the St. Lawrence River to their home. They arrived in Stadacona in September, 1535.

After stopping briefly at Stadacona, Cartier decided to explore farther upriver. He found a second group of Aboriginal Peoples living on an island called Hochelaga. Cartier climbed a nearby hill and named it Mount Royal, or Montreal. He then returned to Stadacona, where he spent the winter with his crew. When Cartier sailed home in the spring, he took Donnacona and his two sons with him. All three Iroquois men died in France.

In 1541, Cartier made his third and final voyage to North America. He left France in May with five ships and 1,500 people. He hoped to start a settlement on the St. Lawrence River. Cartier and the **settlers** succeeded in building a camp on the river, but over the course of the winter, many of the settlers died. Cartier's plan to start a settlement had failed. He sailed back to France in June 1542. More than 60 years passed before French explorers travelled to the area again.

How Canada Was Named

When Cartier returned to North America in 1535, Donnacona's sons, Domagaya and Taignoagny, travelled with him. As the ship neared their home, the young men pointed in the direction of their settlement and told Cartier they were on the road to *kanata*. Kanata was the Iroquois word for village. Cartier thought they had said Canada. He thought that this was the name of Donnacona's settlement and the area around it. Domagaya and Taignoagny were telling Cartier that they were nearing the village of Stadacona. In his journal, Cartier wrote of the village using this name, and called the St. Lawrence River the "rivière du Canada."

The first European map to use the name Canada for the area around the Gulf of St. Lawrence appeared in 1547. Rulers of France often used the word Canada to describe the area that is now Quebec.

Many places in early Canada had names that were given to them by the Aboriginal Peoples before Europeans arrived. **What place names do you know that were named after Aboriginal words?**

WHEN CARTIER CAME TO OUR LAND

Taignoagny was one of Donnacona's sons. He met Cartier on the Gaspé Peninsula in the summer of 1534. This is how Taignoagny might have described his meeting with the newcomers and the first winter Cartier spent at Stadacona. How did Taignoagny and his people help Cartier?

The newcomers built a tall wooden cross and placed it near the water. My father took me, my brother Domagaya, and several others in our canoes to see the cross. We were careful not to get too close to the newcomers' ships. We could see many people standing on the decks.

Father stood up in our canoe. He pointed to the cross and gave a long speech to the newcomers. Then he pointed to the land all around us. He wanted the newcomers to know that the Creator had given the land for all of us to use. The newcomers should have asked him, the chief, if they could use the land too.

Their leader was named Jacques Cartier. He held up an axe. He pretended he wanted to trade the axe for Father's black bearskin robe. When our canoe drew near the ship, some of Cartier's men jumped in. They grabbed us and pulled us on board. They told us with signs that the cross was just a landmark to guide them back to the spot, but I did not believe them.

Cartier gave my brother and me cloth shirts, bright ribbons, and red caps. He put shiny chains around our necks. He gave Father axes and knives.

My brother and I stayed on the ship while everyone else went back to shore in the canoes. At noon the next day, Father returned with some of our people. They brought lots of fish. Father asked Cartier to let us go, but he refused.

The next day, Cartier's ships sailed away. He took us with him. After many days at sea, we landed in Cartier's country. It was called France. We saw many interesting things there. We learned to speak Cartier's language. Everyone we met asked us about our land. "How big is it?" they asked. "Does it have any gold?"

Domagaya and I told them what they wanted to hear because we wanted to go home as quickly as possible. Our answers made many of them eager to see our homeland.

After winter passed, Cartier took us on his ship again. We sailed back across the ocean with two other ships. This time, we helped Cartier find his way back. We guided him to the great river that flowed by our village.

When we reached our home at Stadacona, our people greeted us joyfully. Father thanked Cartier for bringing us back safely. Cartier found a good harbour for his ships not far from the village. He told us he wanted to go farther up the river. He asked us to go with him. Father did not want Cartier to go upriver until he reached a trading agreement with our people. Cartier went anyway. He took about 50 sailors with

him. The rest of his crew stayed behind. They began to build a fort near our village, even though they had not asked us whether they could.

When Cartier came back, he told us he had gone as far as the village of Hochelaga. The people he met at Hochelaga had given him a warm welcome. They brought him fish and corn bread. They invited him to a feast, but he wanted to get back to Stadacona before winter set in and the river froze.

During winter, Cartier's men became sick. Their arms and legs swelled. Their gums hurt, and their teeth became loose. They had a disease called scurvy. Many of them died. Cartier asked us to help him cure his men. Domagaya told Cartier how to make tea from the bark and needles of white cedar trees.

Two women from our village helped Cartier gather some cedar branches. They showed him how to grind the bark and the needles, and how to boil them in water. When the sick people drank the cedar drink, they began to get better. Soon, their health and strength returned.

Now spring has come again. Over the past few weeks, Cartier and his men have been preparing to sail away. Father, Domagaya, and I went to Cartier's fort this morning to say goodbye. Cartier invited us inside, but then he deceived us again. He has forced us onto his ship. He will not let us go, and now the ships are sailing away from the shore. I fear we are going back to France. I do not want to leave my home again.

> Domagaya told Cartier how to make tea from the bark and needles of white cedar trees.

Martin Frobisher

Before Frobisher returned to Great Britain, he captured an Inuk man in his kayak.

Frobisher Strait was renamed after the 1860 discovery that it is actually a bay.

France was not the only European country to maintain an interest in finding a route to Asia. In the sixteenth century, the idea of a Northwest Passage that would open a trade route to the Pacific also intrigued the British. One explorer, Martin Frobisher, was able to convince Queen Elizabeth I that he could reach Asia by sailing northwest around North America. She granted Frobisher permission to explore the area on behalf of Great Britain and ordered some merchants to supply his ships. Frobisher made his first trip in the summer of 1576.

Upon crossing the Atlantic, Frobisher explored the coast of Labrador. From there, he sailed farther north. He came to what he believed was a large strait, which he named Frobisher Strait. His ship then sailed into a narrow channel containing many small islands. Frobisher was convinced that he had found the Northwest Passage.

Once the channel narrowed, however, Frobisher's ship could not travel farther. He and his crew decided to visit a nearby island. There, they met the Inuit who lived along the coast. The Inuit visited Frobisher's ship to trade their sealskins and bearskins for bells, mirrors, and other small items. Using sign language, Frobisher asked one of the group to guide his ship through the passage. The **Inuk** agreed. Five sailors went with the Inuk to get his kayak. They never returned.

Frobisher assumed the Inuk had killed his men. He decided to

return to Great Britain. On his way, he captured an Inuk man in his kayak and brought him back to Europe. He also collected some rock he had found on shore. He thought the rock contained gold. When he arrived in Great Britain, Frobisher showed the rock to some merchants, who agreed to pay for another voyage.

In 1577, Frobisher embarked on his second voyage. He returned to the area he had previously visited and collected more rock. While there, he tried to find out what had happened to the five sailors who had disappeared the previous year. One day, he found an empty tent that he thought might belong to the men. His crew tried to catch a group of Inuit to ask about the tent. The Inuit attempted to escape in their kayaks, but Frobisher's men rowed after them, and a fierce battle took place. Some of the Inuit were killed. Shortly after, Frobisher and his crew returned to Great Britain.

FURTHER UNDERSTANDING

Iron Pyrite

Iron pyrite is a type of **mineral**. It has a golden color, which often causes people to mistake it for gold. For this reason, iron pyrite is sometimes called "fool's gold." One way to tell if a rock is iron pyrite or gold is to strike it with a hammer. Iron pyrite will spark. As a result, it can be used to start fires. Iron pyrite also produces a foul odour when heated. True gold does not.

Queen Elizabeth I granted Martin Frobisher permission to sail on behalf of Great Britain.

Frobisher returned to North America a third time in 1578. He brought 15 ships to haul tonnes of rock back to Great Britain. There, he was devastated to learn that the rock was not gold, but iron pyrite. It was worthless.

Frobisher never found out what happened to the five missing sailors. Three hundred years later, an American explorer heard an Inuit story about five Europeans who had come with the first ships. These men lived with the Inuit for a few years. Then they built a large boat and sailed out into the open water. The Inuit never saw them again.

Samuel de Champlain

Samuel de Champlain was a French explorer and mapmaker. He made many of the first drawings and maps of North America. His records provided the first detailed accounts of the region since Cartier's voyages 60 years earlier.

In 1603, Champlain joined a trading expedition to the St. Lawrence region. He sailed up the St. Lawrence River. When his ship could not travel any farther, he asked the local **Algonquian** peoples what lay beyond. They told him of a great lake filled with salty water. Champlain returned to France convinced he had discovered a route to Asia.

In France, Champlain told King Henry IV about his discoveries. The next year, Henry IV sent Champlain and his business partner, Pierre Du Gua Sieur de Monts, to found a colony in the French area of North America called New France. Champlain and de Monts sailed to the Bay of Fundy with about 80 settlers. There, they built a colony called Port-Royal.

Until 1606, Champlain stayed at Port-Royal and continued to explore the Atlantic coast. He briefly returned to France but was put in charge of a new expedition in 1608. Once again, he sailed up the St. Lawrence River. At a spot along the shore that was protected

Samuel de Champlain was born in France in 1570 and died in Quebec in 1635.

by cliffs, Champlain built a fur trading post. He called the post Quebec, after the Aboriginal word for the area, *kebec*, meaning "where the river gets narrow." The settlement became the capital of New France. Today, it is one of the oldest cities in North America.

After founding Quebec, Champlain continued to search for the Northwest Passage. In 1615, he undertook a voyage in search of a route west to a sea some Aboriginal Peoples had told him about. During the voyage, Champlain reached Lake Huron, where he met the Huron people. From there, he headed southeast, where he discovered Lake Ontario. Champlain was disappointed because neither of these lakes was the Pacific Ocean.

After this trip, Champlain never explored again. However, near the end of his life, Champlain used all he had learned from his own trips and those of other explorers to draw a map of North America. This map was the first to show the rivers and lakes of eastern Canada in detail, and presented everything that was known about North America at the time. After Champlain's death, the map helped many others explore the area.

▲▲▲▲▲ FIRST-HAND ACCOUNT

The Order of Good Cheer

Champlain and his men spent the winter of 1605 at Port-Royal. To cope with the difficult conditions, Champlain created *L'Ordre de Bon Temps,* or the Order of Good Cheer. According to the Order, crew members took turns cooking meals for the entire company. They also provided entertainment and fun in the form of plays and dancing:

We spent this winter very pleasantly, and had good fare by means of the Order of Good Cheer which I established, and which everybody found beneficial to his health, and more profitable than all sorts of medicine we might have used. This order consisted of a chain which we used to place with certain little ceremonies about the neck of one of our people, commissioning him for that day to go hunting. The next day it was conferred upon another, and so on in order. All vied with each other to see who could do the best, and bring back the finest game. We did not come off badly, nor did the Indians who were with us.

Samuel de Champlain started the Order of Good Cheer to keep up the spirits of his crew during the long, cold winter.

People With Different Ideas

Each group had different ideas about how Champlain should spend his time.

Champlain worked with many groups of people while he lived in Canada. Each group had different ideas about how he should spend his time. Sometimes their ideas were in conflict.

A French Merchant

I gave Champlain money to pay for his voyages. I paid for his ships, his crew, and his supplies. The only way I can get my money back is from the sale of furs.

I want Champlain to spend his time trading for furs so he can repay my loan. He cannot do that if he is always exploring, or if he is back in France looking for more settlers.

A Quebec Settler

I came to this new land to farm with my husband and children. Before we moved here, Champlain promised to help us clear the land to grow crops. He said that other

Fur from beaver and other animals was used as decorative trim on clothing and hats. When silk became popular, the demand for fur dropped.

FURTHER UNDERSTANDING

The Fur Trade

The main purpose of European settlements in early Canada was to make money. One of the ways this happened was through trade with Aboriginal Peoples. Almost as soon as the two groups came into contact, Europeans began trading tools and weapons with Aboriginal Peoples in exchange for furs from animals such as the beaver. These furs were very easy to sell in Europe, since they were used to make hats and other clothing. The fur trade quickly became a very important part of the economy in early Canada.

settlers would join us, but only a few have come so far. We want him to keep his promises.

We also need Champlain to build a strong fort at Quebec. We are afraid that our settlement might be attacked by the British and the Iroquois. The Iroquois are the **allies** of the British and the enemies of our Aboriginal trading partners. We need Champlain to defend Quebec and help it grow.

A French Official

We sent Champlain to North America to search for a route to Asia. We want him to keep exploring until he finds it. We also want him to help run the settlement he has started. He knows the people and the land better than anyone, so he can act as governor and judge.

We expect that Champlain will send new maps and drawings showing us what he has seen. We want him to write reports about all his activities and send them to us in France.

Champlain's colony at Quebec suffered a severe winter during its first year. Of 32 colonists, only 9 survived.

Henry Hudson

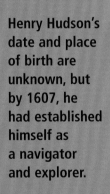

While Champlain was establishing permanent colonies in New France, the British continued to search for a western route to Asia. In 1609, explorer Henry Hudson set out from Great Britain to find the Northwest Passage. Two years earlier, Hudson had tried to sail to Asia by way of the North Pole. This time, he tried a different direction. Hudson and his crew sailed west across the Atlantic Ocean to North America. He sailed his ship, the *Half Moon*, up a river that begins where the city of New York is today. When Hudson realized the river was not the Northwest Passage, he returned to Great Britain. Today, the river is called the Hudson River.

In April 1610, Hudson and his crew again set sail in search of the Northwest Passage. This time, with Frobisher's maps to help him, Hudson sailed northwest into Arctic waters. After sailing through a narrow strait filled with ice, he entered a large, open body of water. He followed the coast that bordered the water. Hudson thought he had reached the west coast of North America. In fact, he had discovered a large bay that was later named Hudson Bay.

After months of searching for a way out of the bay, Hudson's ship, the *Discovery*, was blocked by land. With winter coming, Hudson and his crew landed. They spent the winter on the shore near their boat. The weather was terrible. Supplies ran low, and the sailors became ill with scurvy.

After a long winter, spring finally arrived. As soon as the ice melted and the ship was free to sail, the crew wanted to return home. Hudson did not agree. He wanted to continue the search for the Northwest Passage. Angry and starving, the crew **mutinied**. They set Hudson, his son, and some loyal crew members adrift in a small boat. They were never seen again.

Although Hudson did not find the Northwest Passage, his explorations later helped Great Britain lay claim to the area around Hudson Bay. This area became very important to the fur trade, since it allowed the British to transport furs from Hudson Bay to Great Britain.

Mutiny Aboard the *Discovery*

One of the men who sailed with Hudson was his 19-year-old son John. If John had kept a journal of his trip, it might have been similar to the following passage.

April 17, 1610
We set sail today, heading west. Father is sure we will be the first to reach China using this route.

June 16
Yesterday ice nearly crushed our ship. The ice was so close I could almost touch it. The men are worried, but father wants to keep sailing.

July 27
We are away from the ice now. There is open sea and the weather is warm. Father says we are close to China.

August 29
We still have not found China. It's getting colder again. The land is rocky and empty.

September 20
Father has decided to stop for the winter. The crew are building a shack on shore. I am freezing. Ice is forming around the ship.

December 8
Many men are sick. The carpenter died today. The crew fought over who would get his coat.

June 18
I am so happy! Our ship is finally free of the ice and we are almost ready to set sail.

June 20
I heard the men grumbling last night. They think Father is hiding food from them. They no longer want to explore.

June 23
The crew took over the *Discovery* today. They ordered Father, me, and some other crew members to get into the small boat. Then they sailed away. What will happen to us?

British Explorers in the Arctic

By 1650, the search for the Northwest Passage was abandoned.

The achievements of British explorers Martin Frobisher and Henry Hudson opened early Canada's Far North for further exploration. British explorers who followed pushed the search for a Northwest Passage into the icy waters of the Canadian Arctic.

In 1612, Sir Thomas Button led an expedition along the northeast coast of North America and into northern Arctic waters. Button's expedition set sail from Great Britain in two vessels, the *Resolute* and Henry Hudson's old ship, the *Discovery*. So confident was Button that he would find the Northwest Passage to the Far East that he carried with him a personal letter from King James I addressed to the emperor of Japan. Button failed in his mission, but he was able to chart the west coast of the Hudson Bay as far as the Nelson River.

Other seafarers continued the search. Robert Bylot and his navigator, William Baffin, made several exploration voyages to the North in the early seventeenth century. In 1616, they discovered Baffin Bay. Within a few years, they were followed by Luke Foxe, who discovered Foxe Channel in 1631.

While none of these explorers found the Northwest Passage, their voyages helped chart the eastern Arctic waters of the Far North. By 1650, the British abandoned the search for the Northwest Passage. Instead, the rulers of Great Britain focussed their attention on the settlement of North America's interior. The search for the Northwest Passage did not resume until the early nineteenth century, when charts and maps from these early years of exploration were put back into use. The Northwest Passage was not sailed from east to west until 1905, when Roald Amundsen from Norway finally completed the voyage.

The efforts of early explorers in the Arctic led to the Northwest Passage finally being travelled in 1903.

HOW TO USE AN ATLAS

Most early European explorers discovered North America while looking for a shorter route to Asia. To understand the history of early Canadian exploration, historians must be able to read and interpret the information found in maps.

Historians must be able to read and interpret the information found in maps.

Voyages of Exploration to the New World

Name	Date	Accomplishment
Christopher Columbus	1492	Claimed West Indies
John Cabot	1497	Visited what is now Newfoundland and Labrador
João Fernandes	1499	Reached Labrador
Gaspar Corte-Real	1501	Landed in what is now Newfoundland and Labrador
Giovanni da Verrazzano	1524	Cruised the east coast of America
Jacques Cartier	1534–41	Explored the Gulf of St. Lawrence
Samuel de Champlain	1603–15	Explored the St. Lawrence region

Voyages of Exploration to the Canadian Arctic

Name	Date	Accomplishment
Martin Frobisher	1576	Sailed into Frobisher Bay
Henry Hudson	1610	Explored Hudson Bay
Thomas Button	1612	Explored the coast of Hudson Bay
William Baffin	1616	Mapped Baffin Bay
Luke Foxe	1631	Sailed into Foxe Channel

On your own or with a partner:

Research the starting points of the voyages listed in the chart. Using an atlas, trace the voyages from their starting points to the discovery points. How far did the explorers sail?

In a small group:

Discuss what maps show about the physical and climatic conditions of each location. Brainstorm how these conditions could have affected the success or failure of voyages to these places.

TIMELINE

Events of the past can be shown on timelines. This timeline shows the years 1000 through 1791.

1000
The Norse sail to North America for the first time.

1003
Thorvald Eriksson, a Norse explorer, encounters a group of Aboriginal Peoples in Canada.

1400
European merchants use overland routes to trade with Asia.

1440
New instruments and better maps help sailors find their way across oceans and seas.

1480
The search begins for a sea route to Asia. Some people sail east around Africa. Others sail west across the Atlantic.

1497
Explorer John Cabot reaches the Grand Banks near what is now Newfoundland.

1510
Fishers from Europe begin annual visits to the Grand Banks.

1520
Fishers begin to trade with Aboriginal Peoples along the eastern coast of North America.

1534
Explorer Jacques Cartier explores the Gulf of St. Lawrence and claims the area for the king of France.

1560
Hats made from beaver fur become fashionable in Europe.

1576
Explorer Martin Frobisher explores the coast of what is now Labrador and sails to Frobisher Bay by Baffin Island.

1605
The French start a settlement at Port-Royal. Explorer Samuel de Champlain begins a settlement at Quebec.

1610
Explorer Henry Hudson sails into Hudson Bay. The Huron help Champlain explore inland areas. French farmers settle in the St. Lawrence River valley.

1611

Jesuit missionaries come to Canada to teach Christian beliefs to the Aboriginal Peoples.

1639

Ursuline nuns come to Quebec.

1642

Ville-Marie is founded as a mission post on the island of Montreal.

1649

The Iroquois, Aboriginal allies of the British, wipe out the Huron, Aboriginal allies of the French, in a war for control of the fur trade.

1659

Radisson and Groseilliers explore the area northwest of the Great Lakes.

1670

The Hudson's Bay Company is formed by the British.

1691

Explorer Henry Kelsey reaches the Prairies and sees buffalo.

1713

The Treaty of Utrecht gives Great Britain control over part of eastern Canada and the land around Hudson Bay.

1731

Pierre Gaultier de Varennes et de la Vèrendrye begins exploring west of the Great Lakes and the Prairies.

1750

The British build a fortress at Halifax.

1755

The British expel the French settlers, called Acadians, from Nova Scotia.

1756

The Seven Years' War begins in Europe and spreads to North America.

1758

The French complete construction of Louisbourg, a fortress on Île Royale.

1760

The British destroy the French fortress at Louisbourg.

1763

The Treaty of Paris ends the Seven Years' War. Great Britain takes control of eastern Canada.

1774

The Quebec Act lets French settlers keep their language, religion, and some of their laws.

1783

The American colonies become the United States. Loyalist settlers from the United States move to eastern Canada.

1791

The Constitutional Act divides Quebec into two provinces—Upper Canada and Lower Canada.

HOW TO USE MAPS OF HISTORICAL SITES

Historians cannot always visit the actual location of a place they are studying. Maps of historical and archaeological sites can give us clues about the lifestyle of people who lived there. Use the map of the Norse settlement at L'Anse aux Meadows to work through Steps 1–5.

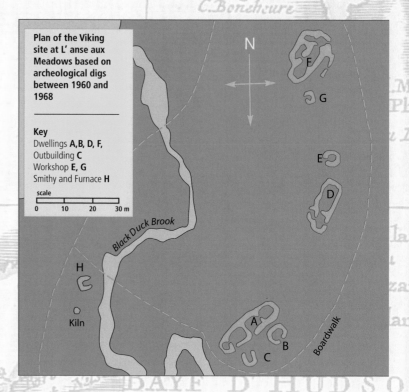

Plan of the Viking site at L' anse aux Meadows based on archeological digs between 1960 and 1968

Key
Dwellings **A, B, D, F,**
Outbuilding **C**
Workshop **E, G**
Smithy and Furnace **H**

scale
0   10   20   30 m

Step 1

Carefully review the information provided in the key to the map. Note the type and location of all the structures. Make notes of what you know about the Norse settlement from the map. How many people might have lived there?

Step 2

Make a two-column chart in your notebook. In the left column, list the basic needs of the settlers. In the right column, suggest ways the settlers might have met each need. Are there any needs they might not be able to meet?

Step 3

The buildings at L'Anse aux Meadows do not include a barn for farm animals.

What does this suggest about life in the settlement? What other types of buildings are absent? Why? Why were the buildings shown built at those specific locations?

Step 4

Using the information from the map, write a description of an average day at the settlement. What were the daily activities of the settlers? What did they eat? Be as descriptive as possible given the data you gather from the map.

Step 5

Research the Norse settlement at L'Anse aux Meadows to find out how accurate you were in your portrayal of daily life.

TWO CULTURES MEET

When Cartier sailed into the Bay of Chaleur in July 1534, he and his crew saw about 40 canoes in the distance. The people in the canoes were Mi'kmaq who lived along the coast in the Maritimes. The Mi'kmaq held up furs on sticks and made signs for the French to come ashore. Cartier recorded his impression of the meeting in his journal.

But as we were only one boat we did not care to go, so we rowed towards the other fleet which was on the water. And they [on shore], seeing we were rowing away, made ready two of their largest canoes in order to follow us. These were joined by five more of those that were coming in from the sea, and all came after our long-boat, dancing and showing many signs of joy, and of their desire to be friends, saying to us in their language: "Napou tou daman asurtat," and other words we did not understand. But for the reason already stated, that we had only one of our long-boats, we did not care to trust their signs and waved to them to go back, which they would not do but paddled so hard that they soon surrounded our long-boat with their seven canoes. And seeing that no matter how much we signed to them, they would not go back, we shot off over their heads with two small cannons. On this they began to return towards the point, and set up a marvellously loud shout, after which they proceeded to come on again as before. And when they had come alongside our long-boat, we shot off two fire-lances which scattered among them and frightened them so much that they began to paddle off in very great haste, and did not follow us any more.

What do you think?

1. Why did Cartier not want to meet with the Mi'kmaq? What would suggest that Cartier was not the first European the Mi'kmaq had seen?
2. Write an account of this event from the point of view of the Mi'kmaq.
3. Work in a small group to role play the scene described by Cartier. What communication problems occurred? How might they have been avoided?
4. How can language problems be overcome?

FURTHER RESEARCH

How can I learn more about Canada's early explorers?

Libraries

Most libraries have computers that connect to a database for searching for information. If you input a key word, you will be provided with a list of books in the library that contain information on that topic. Non-fiction books are arranged numerically, using their call number. Fiction books are organized alphabetically by the author's last name.

Internet Resources

The Internet can be an excellent source of information. For more reliable results, look for websites created by government agencies, non-profit organizations, and educational institutions. Online encyclopedias can also be a great source. Avoid personal web pages or sites that are trying to sell something.

Canada: A People's History Online

history.cbc.ca
The online companion to CBC's award-winning television series on the history of Canada, as told through the eyes of its people. This multimedia website features behind-the-scenes information, games and puzzles, and discussion boards. It is also available in French.

The Canadian Encyclopedia Online

www.thecanadianencyclopedia.com
A reference for all things Canadian. In-depth history articles are accompanied by photographs, paintings, and maps. Articles can be read in both French and English.

GLOSSARY

Aboriginal Peoples: the first people who lived in Canada, and those who are descended from them, including First Nations, Inuit, and Métis

Algonquian: Aboriginal Peoples of the Eastern Subarctic

allegiance: loyalty to a ruler

allies: people or nations who help each other

astrolabe: astronomical instrument that was once used to measure the Sun and the stars to determine location; was replaced by the sextant

colony: a settlement created by people who have left their own country to settle in another land

documents: something written or printed that provides proof of a fact

holds: storage areas below the deck of a ship

Inuk: refers to one member of the Inuit group

masts: long, upright, wooden poles that support the sails and rigging of a ship

merchants: people who buy goods and sell them for higher prices

Middle Ages: a period in European history extending from the fifth century to the beginning of the Renaissance

mineral: a natural substance that is neither plant nor animal

monarchs: people who rule countries, such as queens and kings

mutinied: rebelled or acted against the orders of a leader

Norse: people of ancient Scandinavia

peninsula: a piece of land almost surrounded by water

plundered: stole goods, using force or violence

resources: things that can be used to meet needs

settlers: people who go to live in a different region

sextant: a tool used in navigation to determine latitude and longitude

treaty: a signed agreement between two or more countries

ventilated: supplied with fresh air

INDEX